The Silly Saurus

Written by Lisa Thompson
Paintings by Ritva Voutila

Brock has a little brother named Jock. Jock is a very clumsy dinosaur. He trips over rocks, spills his drinks, and mixes everything up. All the other dinosaurs think Jock is very funny.

Jock tripped over the headland and splashed into the sea. He landed safely in Ellie's underwater garden.

"Thank goodness for sea sponges," giggled Jock.

Ellie smiled.

Jock wanted to join Trio's herd. He dressed up like Trio. Trio's herd thought Jock looked very funny with three horns.

"How can you tell it's me?" asked Jock.

Trio couldn't stop laughing.

Jock wanted to fly like Tickles. He leaped down the mountain.

"Look at me," yelled Jock. "I'm flying, sort of."

Jock leaped and tumbled. He ended up rolling down the mountain.

Tickles laughed and laughed.

Jock tried to start a dinosaur diving contest at the Great Lake.

"Yipppeee, a double dino flip," he squealed.

All the young dinosaurs fell about laughing.

Jock got his party invitations mixed up. He turned up to River's birthday party in fancy dress.

"I thought it was a princess party," said Jock.

Brock was in stitches.

But no one laughed when Jock accidentally fell over a sleeping Rex and woke him up.

"You are a very annoying and silly saurus," yelled Rex. "Give me one good reason why I should not eat you."

"Because I am not as silly as you think I am," said Jock.

"Oh really," said Rex. "Tell me then, what looks the same as you but weighs nothing? If you cannot answer this riddle by sunset, you are a silly saurus and I am going to eat you."

Jock stumbled into the jungle and tried to figure out Rex's riddle. The deeper he walked into the jungle, the darker it grew. The shadows around him became bigger and longer.

The shadows made Jock think.

At sunset, Jock stumbled into his meeting with Rex. Jock slipped over and ran into Rex's tummy.

"Hello silly saurus," said Rex shining his sharp teeth. "I am very hungry."

"That's too bad," said Jock, "because I know what looks the same as me but weighs nothing — MY SHADOW!"

Rex's tummy roared in shock.

"It looks like you're the silly dinosaur who doesn't have any dinner," said Jock, as he skipped and stumbled away.